BRITAIN'S HERITAGE

The Home Front in World War Two

Neil R. Storey & Fiona Kay

AMBERLEY

This book is dedicated to all who served on our Home Front during the Second World War, especially Neil's dear Aunt Dorothy, pictured here in her Women's Land Army uniform in 1944. A true 'Cinderella of the Soil.'

First published 2017

Amberley Publishing
The Hill, Stroud
Gloucestershire, GL5 4EP

www.amberley-books.com

Copyright © Neil R. Storey & Fiona Kay, 2017

The right of Neil R. Storey & Fiona Kay to be identified as the Author of this work has been asserted in accordance with the Copyrights, Designs and Patents Act 1988.

ISBN 978 1 4456 7015 7 (paperback)
ISBN 978 1 4456 7016 4 (ebook)

British Library Cataloguing in Publication Data.
A catalogue record for this book is available from the British Library.

Printed in the UK.

Contents

Introduction

'We shall defend our island, whatever the cost may be. We shall fight on the beaches, we shall fight on the landing grounds, we shall fight in the fields and in the streets, we shall fight in the hills; we shall never surrender.'

Winston Churchill, speech to the House of Commons, 4 June 1940

It's now over eighty years since the storm clouds of the Second World War began to gather over Europe and those who lived through those times and endured the war on the Home Front are sadly beginning to fade away.

I have encountered people who query why we need to remember or even pose the question, 'Why dig that all up again?' I argue sometimes a victory is taken for granted. Britain was not invaded but it was a close-run thing. Make no mistake about it: the orders exist where the Home Guard were told they would defend their positions, if need be, to the last ditch, the last man and the last round of ammunition. The people of countries that were occupied, like France, Belgium and Holland, who experienced life under the heel of the Nazi jackboot and knew what it was to be liberated, teach their children to remember the sacrifices of the past and respect the cost of freedom.

A proud team of Seamen's Christmas Fundraisers at Holy Trinity Church, Hull, winter 1940.

Public shelter trench for the village of Burnham Norton, Norfolk, 1938.

I consider it a privilege to have grown up knowing some of the last of those who served or lived through both world wars and as a historian I have specialised in the study of the impact of twentieth-century warfare on British society for over twenty-five years. During the many lectures and talks I have presented to both student and public audiences, it has become apparent to me that some of the things I and other historians accepted as common knowledge when we began are no longer well-known. As time passes it also appears that the 'popular memory' of the Second World War handed down to future generations has frequently become blurred; erroneous assumptions have been made, generalisations are rife and the contribution of some civilian organisations to the war effort and to those suffering as a direct result of the war are all but forgotten.

This book does not set out to be an encyclopaedic tome but I hope it will provide a timely and useful volume for anyone approaching the subject for the first time, those researching local or family history or wishing to obtain a concise overview of the topic filled with handy facts, statistics and stories about the British Home Front.

There is no glory in war but what I hope emerges in telling this story is something of the spirit of the times, the good humour, hard work, selflessness, kindness and fortitude that brought the British people though their darkest hours during the Second World War.

Neil R. Storey

1

The Road to War

As Hitler and the Nazi Party gained power in Germany, fears over the regeneration of German aggression in the air were confirmed with the official establishment of the German Air Force, the Luftwaffe, in February 1935. In September that same year British Prime Minister Stanley Baldwin issued a circular entitled *Air Raid Precautions* (ARP) that invited local authorities to set up working committees and undertake measures, such as the construction of public shelters to protect the populace. Most county councils established ARP committees but very few went so far as to construct any shelters. It took events during the Spanish Civil War and the international horror after the bombing of Madrid in November 1936 to galvanise the active development of air raid precautions in Britain. That same month the British government created the Air Raid Wardens Service and emergency services were holding their first ARP training courses.

The *Air Raid Precautions Handbook No 1: Personal Protection Against Gas* was published in 1936. Local authorities would ask the St John Ambulance and Red Cross to help by going about their local town or village to explain the dangers of poison gas, and air raids in general, and to suggest how simply those dangers could be avoided. In practice, however, there was a lack of detailed planning and cohesion: this was blamed on the lack of official information and guidelines. The bombing of Guernica, Spain, in April 1937 drove forward the development of Britain's air raid precautions. Britain felt vulnerable; our mass population

German airship *Graf Zeppelin* over the British coast, 1931.

centres were based around industrial zones and speculations based on the events in Spain generated warnings of 'knock out blows' with some 9 million people exposed to air attack the moment war broke out. Estimates conjectured that if bombing continued over sixty days as many as 600,000 would be killed and 1,200,000 injured and mass panic would ensue. It was further suggested that 100,000 tons of bombs could be dropped on London alone in the first fourteen days, a figure that would exceed the total quantity of explosives dropped on the city during the entire war. But over the years 1937–39 it was taken very seriously and thousands of emergency compressed cardboard coffins were issued to Casualty Clearing Services across the country for the anticipated air-raid casualties.

The first Air Raid Precautions Bill was brought before Parliament in late 1937; by the end of the year the ARP organisation had recruited over 200,000 volunteers nationally, Chief Wardens had been appointed, the initial national structure of the ARP organisation was in place and a number of local areas had produced their first ARP schemes.

Early in 1938 Stella Isaacs, the Dowager Marchioness of Reading, was asked by the government to form the Women's Voluntary Services for Air Raid Precautions. By May 1938 it had been established with the objectives of 'the enrolment of women for Air Raid Precaution Services of Local Authorities, to help to bring home to every household what air attack may mean, and to make known to every household in the country what it can do to protect itself and the community.' The organisation was designed so that no woman held a rank at a local level, the appointment of 'group leader' being assigned to the most able and appropriate women for the duration of a particular task or project. There was no compulsory uniform; members of the WVS could perform their duties wearing their lapel badge but many chose to buy the approved uniform.

The Munich Crisis of September 1938 saw British Prime Minister Neville Chamberlain fly to Germany to meet with Adolf Hitler. Few believed Chamberlain's declaration on his return of 'Peace for our Time' but what he had done was to buy Britain some time to prepare for war. By the time of his return every man, woman and child in Britain had been issued a gas mask, and a booklet advising how to protect your home against air raids had been delivered to every household. A million feet of air-raid shelter trenches had been dug, the Observer Corps had had its first general call-out, the emergency services had been placed on standby and the first pilot for the government's evacuation scheme was staged.

London County Council drafted plans for the evacuation of 637,000 children from London while other measures were in draft for Britain's industrial cities. In the event around 5,000 children were evacuated under this scheme. By early 1939 all the children from the pilot evacuation had returned home. In January and February 1939 local authorities in Evacuee Reception Areas began the search for potential foster homes. Volunteers – described as 'Visitors' – interviewed householders and filled in census forms. These returns were to help decide how many evacuees could be billeted in each area.

The Home Office booklet *The Protection of Your Home Against Air Raids* was sent to every British household in 1938.

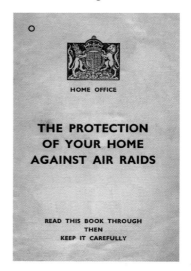

HOME OFFICE

THE PROTECTION OF YOUR HOME AGAINST AIR RAIDS

READ THIS BOOK THROUGH
THEN
KEEP IT CAREFULLY

A working party of volunteers assembling gas masks before distribution to the populace.

Wills's Air Raid Precautions cigarette cards in their album showing how to wear the Civilian and Civilian Duty gas masks.

The ARP schemes and organisation for most towns and villages were in place by early 1939. Members of the public were becoming familiar with the concept and need for ARP; many had attended lectures given at most of the extant civilian-uniformed organisations. Teachers were given a series of lectures on ARP with a special focus on the treatment of children in case of an emergency. Places for the populace to shelter underground had also been identified and construction commenced in cities and towns across the country.

The preparations and recruitment of military forces had been restricted by the War Office and expansion was only permitted in 1939. Many officers felt such things really had been left to 'the eleventh hour'. Full expansion of the Territorial Army (TA) was only ordered on 2 March 1939, when it was announced that the size of the TA was to be doubled, and the major recruitment drive for RAF and RAFVR personnel to fly, crew and maintain the planes did not occur until July 1939.

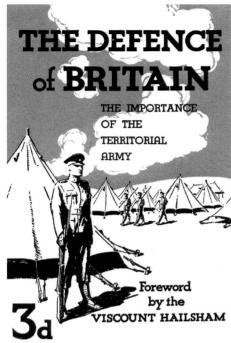

Above left: Programme for the last Empire Air Day, held at RAF stations across Britain, on Saturday, 20 May 1939.
Above right: *The Defence of Britain* with foreword by Viscount Hailsham, Secretary of State for War (1931–35).

Britain's first peacetime act of conscription was passed by Parliament on 26 May. The Military Training Act of 1939, often referred to as 'The Militia Act', applied to all males aged between twenty and twenty-one and required the 35,000 men in this age bracket to answer a compulsory call-up to serve for six months' full-time military training. After this it was stated they would be transferred to the Reserve for three-and-a-half years, during which time they 'might be recalled in an emergency for full-time duty'. In reality most of these lads, commonly known as 'Militiamen', were still in uniform when war broke out and they were in 'for the duration'.

Did you know?

The summer of 1939 saw the emergency services gear up for war. The first practice blackouts were staged between the hours of 12 midnight and 4 a.m. in July 1939. The RAF also conducted a major national air defence exercise from 9 to 11 August. It was the first full practice for the modern air defence system, including fighter and bomber squadrons, anti-aircraft divisions, air-raid warning organisations and the Observer Corps.

A 1938 hallmarked silver Air Raid Precautions badge.

Fire watchers from a large department store, 1940. Other large organisations such as cathedrals, offices, factories and timber merchants were among the first to raise their own teams to equip and train to combat the fire bomb menace.

Norwich City Engineers' Department ARP Decontamination Squad, 1939.

The summer weather of 1939 was glorious and many people did make an extra effort to have a holiday, even if it was just a day trip to the seaside. The military presence and activities in coastal areas increased and the practice gunfire from the anti-aircraft camps thundering over the beaches was an unwelcome reminder of the impending war. Across the country people entered into preparations for war. Training was essential; the ARP presented public lectures on Air Raid Precautions and the British Red Cross Society and St John Ambulance Brigade staged thousands of public First Aid and Home Nursing courses. Council workmen were joined by volunteers of all ages, filling sandbags and building up blast walls for public buildings from town halls and police stations to hospitals, wardens' posts and private homes. Education Committees began the construction of trench shelters for their schools and further works were carried out digging out the trenches for public shelters, factories and businesses at many locations across the country. Some families also dug their own improvised outdoor trench shelters in their back gardens.

The first batch of Anderson shelters reached provincial cities in late August 1939. These shelters were supplied free to all homes with an income that did not exceed £250 a year, if they had a suitable garden. Made from pre-formed corrugated sheet-steel, the Anderson was supplied in twenty-one pieces with a bag of nuts and bolts. The householders and helpful neighbours would join together to dig out the ground, assemble the shelter and pile a good lot of earth back on top. Household shelters were supplemented in cities and towns with public shelters both above and below ground. Britain was gearing up for war and for many in that sunny August of 1939, it was not a matter of if but when hostilities would be declared.

A newly dug-in Anderson Shelter at Two Ball Lonnen, Fenham, Newcastle, 1939. (Newcastle Library)

2

Evacuate!

On 24 August 1939 schoolteachers were recalled from their summer holidays and were thrown in at the deep end preparing for the 'go' signal for Operation Pied Piper – the mass evacuation of vulnerable civilians from bombing target areas to safe areas of the countryside. On 27 August notifications were received by Billeting Officers stating the numbers of children that would be sent to be re-homed in their area and on 31 August 1939 the order 'Evacuate Forthwith' was sent out by the Ministry of Health.

Did you know?

Friday, 1 September 1939 saw the greatest human evacuation in the history of the British Isles. The total numbers evacuated are truly remarkable: 827,000 schoolchildren; 524,000 mothers with children under school age; 103,000 schoolteachers and helpers; 13,000 expectant mothers and 7,000 people with disabilities.

DETAILS OF FACILITIES ARRANGED FOR

(1) OFFICIAL PARTIES
(TO BILLETS PROVIDED BY THE GOVERNMENT)

Evacuation is available for

SCHOOL CHILDREN
MOTHERS with CHILDREN of School Age or under
EXPECTANT MOTHERS

(2) ASSISTED PRIVATE EVACUATION

A free travel voucher and billeting allowance are provided for

CHILDREN OF SCHOOL AGE or under
MOTHERS with CHILDREN OF SCHOOL AGE OR UNDER
EXPECTANT MOTHERS
AGED and BLIND PEOPLE
INFIRM and INVALIDS

who have made their own arrangements with relatives or friends for accommodation in a safer area

* FOR INFORMATION ASK AT THE NEAREST SCHOOL

ISSUED BY THE MINISTRY OF HEALTH

From as early as 6.30 a.m. on 1 September children began to gather in their school playgrounds ready to depart. None of them knew where they were going, who they would be staying with or when they would return. It is true to say the journey of evacuees from across the country varied in duration, incidents, experiences and emotions felt at the time, but it went like clockwork with no major incidents or disasters. To get a flavour of the day, here is a 'typical' evacuee child's journey from London to Norfolk.

After gathering in the school playground, one of the 1,589 assembly points in London, each child (clutching a suitcase, pillowslip or brown parcel of their prescribed items to take with them) would have had a luggage label affixed to them usually bearing their name, school, current home address and number allotted to their evacuation party

Evacuation notice, 1939.

Ready for the off! Evacuees with their gas masks, clothes and personal effects packed into pillowcases.

(usually their school). They may well have been joined there by Evacuation Officers wearing 'L.C.C. EVAC.' marked armbands; their job was to ensure safe passage and that all suitable paperwork regarding numbers was maintained and exchanged; mostly it fell to the council education officers and teachers to take on this role but there were also volunteers.

The children were then moved out, some marching behind the banner or placard of their school all the way to their local station, singing as they went; others piled onto transport, usually buses, coaches, local trains or the Underground, to one of the capital's 168 Entraining Stations – mostly main line stations or suburban stations in outer London such as New Cross, Richmond or Ealing Broadway – and there they would depart for the countryside. Thousands of London children were also brought to the eastern counties on steamers from the Thames, disembarking at Felixstowe, Claremont Pier in Lowestoft and at the Fish Wharf in Great Yarmouth. Some parents managed to follow the children to the departure points and tearfully wave them off. For most children it was a long journey; some had never ridden on a train before and in carriages without corridors the excitement and/or distress led to 'little wet accidents', while those on boats, many of whom had never even seen the sea before, suffered seasickness; however, despite this being the greatest and most concentrated mass movement of people in the history of Great Britain, there were no serious accidents recorded.

Ahead of the children, the towns and villages across the county had been involved in what the local press hailed as 'perhaps the biggest co-operative effort ever made by the government, the local authorities, and the public of Norfolk'. The provisions that had been sent for the children were stated to have included 976 cases of tinned milk, 21,000 lb of biscuits, 73,000 cases of chocolate and 21,000 carrier bags. There had also been an appeal for at least 12,000 blankets and rugs for children being housed temporarily at Yarmouth before being sent to rural areas.

Most children arrived at their destinations in daylight, a few in darkness; only upon arrival did they find out where they were. Met by the local Billeting Officer, a further bus or charabanc journey or a walk took them to the reception centre, often a town, church or school hall. Before they were taken inside a nit inspection would have been carried out; children with sore throats were given a gargle, some children were even given a wash and brush up and whole groups of toddlers were bathed in enamel bowls by the waiting volunteers from such organisations as St John Ambulance, the British Red Cross Society, the Women's Voluntary Service or the Women's Institute. Some children were met with no such luxury and remember thanking goodness that someone picked them despite their having wet pants.

The children were then brought into the hall and lined up; the prospective foster parents would choose the child they wanted. Although attempts were made to keep siblings together, this was not always possible. Who will pick me, I wonder what they will be like, I hope I am not last to be chosen, were just a few of the gamut of thoughts that ran through their minds. The pretty little girls and the boys who could be useful around the home or farm were

Evacuees from London arrive in East Anglia, 1 September 1939.

During the 'Phoney War' of 1939 to May 1940, especially at Christmas, many parents retrieved their children from their evacuee homes.

usually chosen first, but there was usually a residue who would be taken door to door among the known likely houses to find them a home. Rates for payment for those giving homes to evacuees were 8s 6d per week for an unaccompanied child; if you took in a family the rate was 5s for each adult and 3s for each child.

During the 'Phoney War' of 1939 and early 1940 many children returned home from evacuation, especially when there was a chance to spend Christmas with their families. When Hitler unleashed his blitzkrieg in 1940 and France fell, there was a second evacuation, especially away from coastal areas where there was a danger of invasion forces landing.

As the war progressed many more children returned home again, only to have to be evacuated from the London area again during the V-weapon attacks in 1944. In April 1945, the government sent out travel arrangement information for the return of evacuees to their homes after the cessation of hostilities. By 12 July 1945, 54,317 evacuees had returned to London. In August 1945 there were still 76,000 evacuated children and adults in reception areas; most of them had no home to return to because it had been destroyed, their parents killed, or they simply did not wish to return. The evacuation scheme was officially terminated in March 1946.

3
Britain Alone

After seven months of the 'Phoney War', the Battle of France began in earnest on 10 May 1940. Hitler had unleashed his blitzkrieg and by 14 May German Army Group A had broken through the Ardennes, swept west towards Sedan and had set its sights towards the English Channel. Army Group B had invaded the Netherlands and advanced west through Belgium. The blitzkrieg sped through the continent with such apparent ease that fears of the fall of Belgium, France and Holland left many in no doubt Britain would face the onslaught next. Particular concerns were shown over the use of German paratroops being dropped in advance of any invasion. Groups of concerned men in towns and villages were already gathering together to discuss how they would defend their homes; they formed irregular units and began patrolling country areas after dark armed with shotguns.

The morning papers of 14 May headlined a 2,000-tank clash north-west of Liege, Holland was swarming with German troops and Queen Wilhelmina had arrived in London as a refugee; that same evening the Dutch Army surrendered. That night Anthony Eden, the newly appointed Secretary of State for War, broadcast his radio appeal for men to join a brand new force – the Local Defence Volunteers.

Concurrent with the Eden broadcast, a telegram was sent by Eden to the Lord Lieutenant of every county stating: 'I am sure that we may count on your co-operation and help in connection with the Local Defence Volunteer Force.' Each Lord Lieutenant was expected to begin the county structure of the LDV by appointing an Area Commander with overall command and organisation responsibility for the county.

Men of the 8th Battalion, Lancashire Fusiliers (TA), who proceeded to France with the 42nd (East Lancashire) Infantry Division, BEF, in 1939.

Did you know?

Local Defence Volunteers poured in, not in the hundreds as anticipated but in their thousands, some reporting at police stations to register before the end of the broadcast, and kept coming through the night and following day; nationally, some 250,000 gave their names in the first twenty-four hours.

'If the Invader Comes', a government leaflet sent to every household during the time of a very real threat of invasion in June 1940.

There was no medical examination but men would have to be 'of reasonable physical fitness' and 'capable of free movement,' previous military service and/or a knowledge of firearms were considered advantageous. Much to the chagrin of many suitable volunteers already serving in the ARP or in the Special Constabulary, they had to be turned down lest the forces they had already been trained with became too depleted. In reality the recruitment terms were flexible; in some small villages men served in both the Home Guards and the ARP.

In these early months of the LDV the training schedule of each battalion varied greatly across the country but drill and marching were common to all. Their first rifle drill was often with broomsticks and what weaponry they had at their disposal at that time. Crucially, the LDV wanted to set to work on the task it had been set. Most Zones and Groups were rapidly established and their primary function of patrolling set up with duty rotas and their call-out alarm system established in the event of an emergency – for most this was to be the ringing of the local church bells but in case this method was prevented by

An army sentry keeps a weather eye over the gap in the beach defences opened for holidaymakers on the August Bank Holiday, 1940.

Issued by the Ministry of Information in co-operation with the War Office and the Ministry of Home Security.

If the
INVADER
comes

WHAT TO DO — AND HOW TO DO IT

THE Germans threaten to invade Great Britain. If they do so they will be driven out by our Navy, our Army and our Air Force. Yet the ordinary men and women of the civilian population will also have their part to play. Hitler's invasions of Poland, Holland and Belgium were greatly helped by the fact that the civilian population was taken by surprise. They did not know what to do when the moment came. *You must not be taken by surprise.* This leaflet tells you what general line you should take. More detailed instructions will be given you when the danger comes nearer. Meanwhile, read these instructions carefully and be prepared to carry them out.

I

When Holland and Belgium were invaded, the civilian population fled from their homes. They crowded on the roads, in cars, in carts, on bicycles and on foot, and so helped the enemy by preventing their own armies from advancing against the invaders. You must not allow that to happen here. Your first rule, therefore, is :—

(1) IF THE GERMANS COME, BY PARACHUTE, AEROPLANE OR SHIP, YOU MUST REMAIN WHERE YOU ARE. THE ORDER IS "STAY PUT ".

If the Commander in Chief decides that the place where you live must be evacuated, he will tell you when and how to leave. Until you

receive such orders you must remain where you are. If you run away, you will be exposed to far greater danger because you will be machine-gunned from the air as were civilians in Holland and Belgium, and you will also block the roads by which our own armies will advance to turn the Germans out.

II

There is another method which the Germans adopt in their invasion. They make use of the civilian population in order to create confusion and panic. They spread false rumours and issue false instructions. In order to prevent this, you should obey the second rule, which is as follows :—

(2) DO NOT BELIEVE RUMOURS AND DO NOT SPREAD THEM. WHEN YOU RECEIVE AN ORDER, MAKE QUITE SURE THAT IT IS A TRUE ORDER AND NOT A FAKED ORDER. MOST OF YOU KNOW YOUR POLICEMEN AND YOUR A.R.P. WARDENS BY SIGHT, YOU CAN TRUST THEM. IF YOU KEEP YOUR HEADS, YOU CAN ALSO TELL WHETHER A MILITARY OFFICER IS REALLY BRITISH OR ONLY PRETENDING TO BE SO. IF IN DOUBT ASK THE POLICE-MAN OR THE A.R.P. WARDEN. USE YOUR COMMON SENSE.

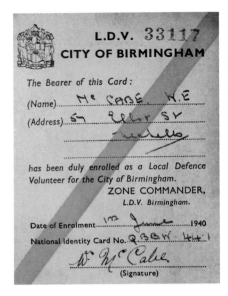

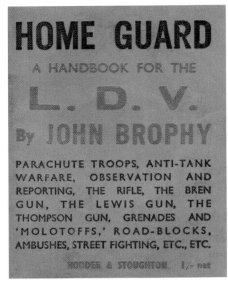

Above left: A Local Defence Volunteer's identity card, 1940. Before uniforms were issued a huge variety of such locally printed cards were issued by LDV units around the country.

Above right: Published in September 1940, *Home Guard: A Handbook for the LDV* was the first of a number of training manuals written specifically for and adopted by the Home Guard by John Brophy.

Below: Home Guards in basic denim uniforms with limited equipment and weaponry tackle a mock armoured car with rifles and 'Molotov cocktails' during an exercise in 1940. Note the concrete anti-tank blocks and railway line sections that obstruct the roadway.

the enemy, a 'knock-list' of manual call-outs was usually agreed and often typed out and distributed to the platoon.

Local invasion committees were set up, designed to co-ordinate the local forces and prepare the defence of their town or village as best as possible in the event of invasion. The population were advised to immobilise vehicles, be they bicycles or motors, when left unattended, hide food supplies and destroy or bury maps or similar materials which might help the enemy. Railway companies issued emergency orders marked 'Secret' which dictated the evacuation of locomotives and rolling stock away from the invasion area and their destruction if they could not be moved. Selected Observer Corps posts in the invasion area were issued with two rifles and ammunition.

There had been fears over the 'Fifth Column' since 1939. These enemy agents and sympathisers were believed to be poised to sabotage the utilities of the country by poisoning water or by blowing up gas works, fouling electricity generating stations and sub stations or cutting telephone lines. Not to mention puncturing tyres of the military and officials, impersonating officers from all armed forces, stealing cars and other motorised vehicles, giving poisoned sweets to children, planting listening devices or 'bugs' all over the place and flashing lights to enemy vessels out to sea or aircraft flying overhead.

Did you know?

Fears about the Fifth Column and traitors tied up much valuable time for the military and the police but most of the 'emergencies' and suspicions were simply concerns from well-meaning, patriotic people and they came to nothing.

A rural village platoon ready to march back from a field exercise in 1941.

Between 26 May and 4 June 1940 the beleaguered British Expeditionary Force (BEF) was evacuated from the beaches of Dunkirk. On 18 June Churchill grimly announced in Parliament: 'What General Weygand called the Battle of France is over. I expect that the Battle of Britain is about to begin.' France capitulated on 25 June and many British households had already received the 'If the Invader Comes' leaflet. The leaflet advised the civilian population to stay put, look out for and report suspicious activity, help our troops and LDV if ordered to do so, hiding maps and immobilizing vehicles, and if you have a factory to organise its defence 'at once.'

On 23 July 1940 Winston Churchill, who had never liked the cumbersome and somewhat ridiculed title of Local Defence Volunteers, saw it formally announced that the organisation be re-named the Home Guard (HG). This was not only a change in name but ushered in a new raft of improvements; structured training, uniform and weaponry supplies and official recognition were set in motion for the million HGs across the country, and established the future of the organisation for the rest of the war.

Churchill's Secret Army

THE GALE & POLDEN
TRAINING SERIES

FIGHTING PATROL
TACTICS

by COL. G. A. WADE, M.C.
Author of "The Defence of Bloodford Village" etc.

Price 1/6 net. by post 1/8

Only ever part of the Home Guard for administrative purposes, one organisation drew on its membership to hand pick men for its very special duties and even adopted HG uniforms to cloak its' members occasional appearances while on manoeuvres or during some of its training with other regular Home Guard units – they were the members of Auxiliary Units, 'Churchill's Secret Army', a top secret organisation whose members, in the event of invasion, were to go to ground, allow the enemy to pass over and then would rise up as a resistance army to harry the army of occupation.

Patrols would only operate in an area within 15 miles of their base and they would have no knowledge of the other units in nearby villages. In the event of a

The *Fighting Patrol Tactics* training manual published by Gale & Polden gave instruction in guerrilla warfare and night operations.

A London taxi cab being used in an anti-aircraft role by Home Guards.

successful invasion and enemy occupation, they were not to communicate in any way with army command, they had to be isolated and autonomous until a successful counter-attack was made or they were wiped out. All Auxiliaries were warned what their operational life expectancy was if there was an invasion – about fifteen days. If they were lucky.

4

'Heroes with Dirty Faces': The Blitz

When war was declared on 3 September 1939, those who had not completed their refuge room or garden shelter set out to finish their tasks. For factories, hospitals and homes to remain operational in the black-out meant that windows would have to be screened or properly fitted with shutters or black-out curtains, no mean feat in any home but the larger premises had hundreds of windows to black out.

The ARP organisation had developed apace and established a structure and specialist 'arms' as shown in the *National Service* booklet (1939):

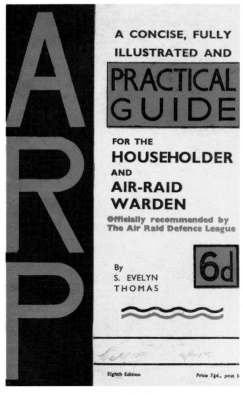

Above left: A Wandsworth Air Raid Warden in his 'Bluette' overalls, tin helmet and gas mask in a bag slung over his shoulder, ready for duty, 1940.
Above right: *ARP: A Practical Guide* booklet for householders and Air Raid Wardens, 1939.

Air Raid Wardens

Rescue (Later further delineated to Rescue (General), and specialist Light Rescue and Heavy Rescue) and Demolition Parties

First Aid Parties

First Aid Posts

Ambulance Drivers and Attendants

Decontamination Squads (Trained to remove all traces of dangerous or persistent gas dropped or sprayed from enemy aircraft from streets, vehicles and buildings)

Report Centres, Communications and Messenger Service

All Air Raid Wardens were trained in anti-gas, basic first aid and elementary fire-fighting techniques and instructed in how to receive, record and send messages. If passed proficient after one month service with their unit, the new warden would be presented with their silver ARP badge. Wardens would also be given a Card of Appointment, signed by the ARP Officer and/or the Clerk to the Local Authority to prove his authority to householders or others he may visit in the course of his duties, and with that a printed armband marked ARP to be worn on the left arm when on duty in civilian clothes. Along with this came their 'appointments' of Civilian Duty Respirator, tin helmet – painted black with a white 'W' for most wardens, while white helmets with diamonds (or later stripes) denoted the more senior ranks among the wardens and ARP Officers – and an ARP-issue whistle suspended from a chain or lanyard to sound and enforce the Air Raid Warning. At the ARP post there would also be a rattle for each warden on duty used to sound the warning in the event of a poison

Testing gas masks are fitted properly in 1939 by placing a disk of card over the filter and asking the wearer to breathe in. If the card was drawn onto the filter, the fit was correct.

Above: Air Raid Wardens, in early 1940. A number are still in civilian clothes and the Chief and District wardens' white helmets display the painted diamonds that denoted rank and were later replaced by black stripes.

Left: The innocent charm and gentle humour of the cover of *Lilliput* magazine, December 1939.

gas attack, and a hand bell to sound and enforce the siren's single rising siren note for 'All Clear'.

The intention of the Warden's Service was to provide a warden's post of five or six wardens for every 400–500 inhabitants. They would also need to know the location of gas mains, electric cables, telephones, shelters and trenches. Wardens would often be first on the scene if air-raid damage had occurred and would be responsible for summoning the proper form of help. Such procedures were rehearsed by staging regular

A charity appeal poster for donations to support the wartime work of the British Red Cross Society and St John Ambulance Brigade.

Give more than ever

RED CROSS
and
S.T JOHN

drills and exercises that also taught the ARP services to work together as a team.

Due to shortages in official supplies, uniforms for ARP Wardens only began to arrive from October 1939. The first issue was that of a 'bluette' light denim overall for men and Macintosh type overcoat for women, with white metal buttons marked ARP. Their dark blue battledress uniforms arrived from 1941.

The Red Cross and St John Ambulance played a key role in Civil Defence, running first-aid posts, training the public in first aid, driving ambulances and providing first aid for air-raid victims. With so many men leaving for war, women were trained as ambulance drivers. They had to learn to drive very quickly, often under blackout conditions, and 'on the job' so as not to

Did you know?

Blackouts not only caused many inconveniences but also led to unprecedented numbers of road traffic accidents; nationally 4,000 people were killed on Britain's roads between September and December 1939; add to that injuries to pedestrians and even fatalities occurring to those left stumbling around the dark streets.

waste petrol. Many of them would attend the aftermath of local air raids and air crashes in the course of their service.

The Auxiliary Fire Service (AFS), founded in 1938, recruited volunteers to supplement the work of established local fire brigades. Each recruit would fill in an application form that was then scrutinised by the Chief Constable. If the man appeared suitable, he would begin training and be issued with a boiler suit, peaked cap and a pair of Wellington boots. Every AFS unit had the authority to requisition or hire either lorries or cars to adapt to tow trailer pumps. By the end of 1938 30,000 auxiliary firemen had been recruited and by the outbreak of war in September 1939 some 89,000 AFS men and 6,000 women were mobilized for full-time service.

Above: Stretcher drill in gas masks for St John Ambulance and Red Cross members, 1940.
Below: Civilian vehicles converted by the Auxiliary Fire Service for the transport of firefighting equipment and to tow fire pumps, 1940.

Above: Auxiliary Fire Service crew and their Coventry Climax fire pump, 1940.
Right: Poster appealing for women to join the National Fire Service, 1941.

During the 'Phoney War,' between late September 1939 and early May 1940, the AFS was seldom needed and was perceived by some as a waste of money and manpower and its male membership stigmatized as 'army dodgers'. As a direct result of this, combined with an increasingly grave situation emerging in France, significant numbers of the AFS began to resign and join other emergency organisations and military services. The government was forced to step in with emergency legislation that 'froze' all firemen in the service. Bombing raids were soon faced by many towns and cities across the country. Whole streets were turned into walls of flame in danger of collapse at any moment, while incredible heat, molten lead dust

Women! You are needed in

THE NATIONAL
FIRE SERVICE
AS FULL-TIME OR PART-TIME MEMBERS

You can train to be a telephonist, despatch rider, driver, canteen worker and for many other duties.

APPLY FOR PARTICULARS TO NEAREST FIRE STATION OR EMPLOYMENT EXCHANGE

and the danger of more bombs falling were constantly faced by the firemen, frequently over successive nights. The public perception of firemen soon changed and they became known as 'the heroes with dirty faces.'

During the Blitz on London the rest of the country did not stand idle and many counties sent pumps and fire crews to assist. When the Blitz spread elsewhere, the same gesture was made but a problem soon emerged because the equipment used by the different brigades was often incompatible and brigades were often found to have different rules and regulations. There were also issues over who was in control. It was clear that fire brigades and AFS units should be unified and as a result all local fire authorities were taken over by the National Fire Service (NFS) in August 1941 and the country was divided into about forty-two fire forces based around geographical areas.

Did you know?

The NFS reached its height in 1942 when there were 100,000 full-time firemen, from a membership of 370,000 personnel, including 80,000 women.

Many servicemen who left a young family at home voiced the opinion that their wives had endured the harder share of the war. Many recalled receiving photographs of those they loved from home and how, although safe and well, they still looked 'war weary'. This is hardly

A Civil Defence Welfare Section, 1941.

surprising; having a home to run, children to care for and with an ever increasing number of food and clothing items being rationed, was quite enough to contend with, but add to that the regular sounding of sirens hailing air raids, false alarms or not, and the fact that with many men leaving factories and businesses more and more women were required to take their place and increase the workforce to fulfil the increased demand for military supplies.

The Blitz

German bombers had conducted mine-laying missions along the British coast in 1939 and as France had fallen more and more enemy raiders bombed our country and soon squadrons of bombers with fighter escorts were darkening our skies during the Battle of Britain. Civilian homes in cities, towns and villages were destroyed and lives were lost through bombing at this time but the aim of these attacks was the destruction of the Royal Air Force (aircraft production factories and airfields) in preparation for invasion.

The Luftwaffe failed to gain air superiority but German intelligence was convinced the last reserve of Fighter Command could be drawn into battle and destroyed if the Luftwaffe turned on London as a primary target. It was also thought by German high command that by bringing London to its knees, British morale would be crippled and that this strategy might even bring the British around to discussing terms. The first major day of the Blitz offensive on London began on 7 September 1940. It was a beautiful summer's day with the sun shining and a clear sky. At 4.35 p.m. the first bombs fell on Ford's motor works at Dagenham, followed by a massive drop of both HE (High Explosive) and incendiary bombs upon Beckton Gas Works, at the time the largest in Europe. Then followed the bombing of the London Docks, factories, warehouses and rows of terraced houses and

The *Handy War-Time Guide for the Woman at Home and the Man in the Street*, one of a wide variety of commercial and government booklets published to verse British society in Air Raid Precautions.

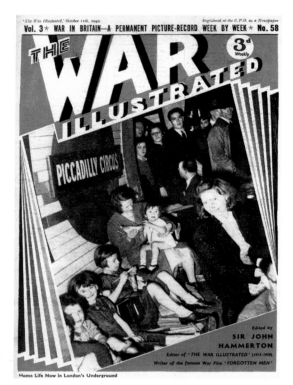

tenements in the East End. Soon the flames and huge columns of greasy black smoke were billowing skyward from Woolwich to Tower Bridge. When the final toll of the day that became known as 'Black Saturday' was counted, 436 men, women and children had been killed and around 1,600 badly injured.

For the next consecutive fifty-seven days London was bombed either during the day or at night. Life during that time could be fraught, dangerous,

Left: *The War Illustrated*, 11 October 1940, with an evocative image of Londoners taking shelter for the night in the London Underground at Piccadilly Circus. Such images were frequently accompanied by the motto: 'London can take it!'
Below: A rare colour image of a blitzed London street with emergency service crews in attendance. In the background can be seen the iconic chimneys of Battersea Power Station. (Science and Society Picture Library)

trying and terrifying, but even without the rosy tint of nostalgia, people really did carry on as best they could. Dramatically, Churchill and the media recorded bold statements such as 'let them all come' and 'we can take it'; these statements certainly caught the spirit of the time and were good for morale. Churchill and other dignitaries came to see the damage for themselves, walking down the blitzed streets and speaking to both emergency service workers and local people. For many in the East End the visit that made the greatest impact upon them was that made by HM King George VI and Queen Elizabeth. A bomb had fallen in the palace quadrangle while their Majesties were in residence, blowing in many of the palace's windows and destroying the chapel. The King and Queen were filmed inspecting their bombed home, the smiling Queen, stoical about the damage inflicted upon her home, thought first of her people and declared: 'I'm glad we have been bombed. It makes me feel I can look the East End in the face.'

People would walk to work down streets still giving off residual heat, smoke and steam as the fire crews damped down burnt buildings. There would be temporary road closures marked by signs and barriers, often attended by a police officer, who would divert people away from a street blocked by debris or rendered dangerous by a broken gas main after bombing. There were also regular instances of unexploded bombs (UXBs), every one of which would require the attendance of a bomb disposal crew. Houses would have to be evacuated, roads closed and if near a railway, the engines would have to be stopped. Many people became so fed up with UXBs that they became quite complacent and if they saw one on the street before the authorities had closed off the area they would move as far

A youngster sits among the rubble of his blitzed London home with the only things he has left: a toy and the clothes he is wearing. (Library of Congress, USA)

YMCA mobile canteen volunteer workers hand out very welcome mugs of tea from their wagon to ARP rescue workers after an air raid.

away as they could from it but would still carry on by. Some would arrive at their place of employment and find it destroyed, burnt out by incendiaries or blasted apart by a direct hit from an HE. Others may well find their shop or premises damaged by the previous night's action, perhaps the shop windows having been blown in, and would help with the clearing up and repairs before they could start work.

The 'Carry On' spirit is all the more remarkable when it is recalled that so many people, after a day at work, would frequently report for duty at a host of wartime organisations like the ARP and WVS. Many others would probably spend an uncomfortable night in an air-raid shelter. Those who were not near their home shelter or did not have their own could use communal street shelters but the provision of these in London at the time of the Blitz was inadequate (it has been argued that this was deliberate as there were those in government who feared that a 'shelter mentality' would develop if people were provided with central deep shelters). Londoners, however, are certainly known for their innovation and notwithstanding the official provisions many started buying platform tickets and spending their nights on the platforms of Underground stations.

A total of seventy-nine underground Tube stations became official public shelters. Shelter marshals were appointed, their duties being to keep order and render first aid if necessary until fully trained assistance arrived. These stations were fitted with bunks to accommodate 22,000 people, were supplied with first-aid facilities and were equipped with chemical toilets. Some 124 canteens also opened across the underground railway system. Conditions in the Underground were frequently cramped; people even slept on the stairs and escalators when they were turned off. Comfort seemed to matter little, nor the conditions that were frequently cold and damp or stifling and smelly. There was no privacy; if you were lucky a loved one would hold a coat around you if you used a communal bucket and woe betide you if it got knocked over! A lesser known phenomenon (because official sources often denied this was happening) that soon became prevalent as the days of the Blitz ran into weeks was 'trekking', whereby thousands of civilians removed themselves from London to sleep outside the capital, travelling several hours into work and several hours out again every day.

In May 1941 Hitler concentrated his efforts towards the Eastern Front and removed his bombers in preparation for the invasion of Russia. The first concentrated blitz on London during the Second World War was over, but that was not the end of the German bombing campaign on Britain. The Blitz on London had destroyed or damaged more than a million houses and more than 20,000 civilians had been killed by bombing in London alone.

The 'Baedeker Blitz'

After the German bombing campaigns failed to destroy airfields and London in 1940–41, Hitler planned to break British morale by attempting to destroy the picturesque and historic cities of England. Spurred by the RAF bombing raids on the historic German cities of Lübeck and Rostock in early 1942, the British cities chosen for the reprisal raids were selected from the German Baedeker tourist guide to Britain. German propagandist Baron Gustav Braun von Sturm is reported to have said after the first attack of the campaign, 'We shall go out and bomb every building in Britain marked with three stars in the Baedeker guide,' and thus the so-called 'Three Star Blitz' or 'Baedeker Blitz' became the name given by the British to these infamous raids on Exeter, Bath, Norwich, York and Canterbury in April–June 1942.

The attacks came with a combination of High Explosive bombs and thousands of incendiaries that rained down. The bombs blasted properties and streets alike, blowing up water mains and utilities, causing the effectiveness of fire engines and

The iconic 'Firebomb Fritz' poster recruiting for the Fire Guard, 1941.

Above: Civil Defence ambulance crews, 1942.
Below: ARP rescue workers, Henderson Hall, Newcastle, 1942. (Newcastle Library)

trailer pumps to be reduced as the water pressure dropped and the fires spread, engulfing whole streets, businesses, churches and pubs. Many people who recall those dreadful nights freely confess they thought that when the daylight came there would be no city left. It is remarkable that none of the cathedrals in these cities were destroyed, although there were many narrow misses and these historic buildings were often saved thanks to the swift actions of volunteer fire guards. Many churches were not so fortunate, as the sheer numbers of incendiary bombs dropped meant they could not be extinguished before they caught fire and then spread. Over 50,000 houses and many other buildings had been left so badly damaged that they were beyond repair. A total of 1,760 people were injured and 1,637 civilians lost their lives during the Baedeker Blitz.

Doodlebugs and Rockets

Air raids on Britain diminished as Hitler ploughed more resources into the Russian Front and other campaigns but even after we gained air superiority after the D-Day landings, it did not mean that the threat from the air was over. Hitler adopted a new strategy to boost German morale and show he could still fight back with jet-powered flying bombs, known in Germany as *Vergeltungswaffe 1* (Vengeance Weapon 1). From mid-June 1944 these weapons were fired at Allied population centres such as Antwerp and London. Only about 25 per cent of these pilotless aircraft hit their intended targets. A combination of defensive measures, mechanical unreliability or guidance errors saw many V1s crash harmlessly into the sea but for the same reasons many of them also landed across the country.

In September 1944 the new V2 long-range rockets were fired at Britain with London as the main target, but there were numerous 'short falls' of V weapons on South East England and it shouldn't be forgotten that there was still the occasional air raid carried out by conventional enemy aircraft right up to 1945.

Girl Guide Rangers (aged fourteen to eighteen) working with the Civil Defence in Norwich, 1944.

5
The Countryside at War

If the coast of Great Britain was where the enemy would have made his landings it was the fields of the countryside where the fighting to stop them would have taken place. 'Stop lines' of pillboxes and fixed defences were soon strung out across our countryside and road blocks manned by soldiers made no road journey along coast or countryside quick or easy – no matter how necessary it was. In June 1940, as France fell and the impending danger of invasion became acute, the British government ordered that all road signs that displayed place names were to be removed and place names on stations or any other property, public or private, should be taken down or obliterated lest they helped any invading forces.

In areas of especial danger of invasion, the local population was evacuated. Some inland estates and farms were requisitioned for military training and for large-scale manoeuvres, especially for tanks and armoured fighting vehicles. This caused a great deal of heartache and in some cases the properties promised to be returned after the war were compulsorily purchased and the farms, hamlets and villages remained a military training area.

The countryside did carry on though – it needed to, to ensure that as the German U-boat campaign claimed thousands of tonnes of merchant shipping, Britain remained able to feed itself. Some key workers on farms were classified as war reserved occupations so even if they tried to enlist, they could not, as many men who had worked on the land or were casually employed from villages at busy times such as harvest had been called up for military service.

Just one month after the outbreak of war the Ministry of Agriculture launched the 'Dig for Victory' scheme that saw private gardens, park land and estates turned into allotments to not only provide essential crops for

DANGER of INVASION

Last year all who could be spared from this town were asked to leave, not only for their own safety, but so as to ease the work of the Armed Forces in repelling an invasion.

The danger of invasion has increased and the Government requests all who can be spared, and have somewhere to go, to leave without delay.

This applies particularly to :—
SCHOOL CHILDREN
MOTHERS WITH YOUNG CHILDREN
AGED AND INFIRM PERSONS
PERSONS LIVING ON PENSIONS
PERSONS WITHOUT OCCUPATION
OR IN RETIREMENT

If you are one of these, you should arrange to go to some other part of the country. You should not go to the coastal area of East Anglia, Kent or Sussex.

School children can be registered to join school parties in the reception areas, and billets will be found for them.

If you are in need of help you can have your railway fare paid and a billeting allowance paid to any relative or friend with whom you stay.

If you are going, go quickly.

Take your
NATIONAL REGISTRATION IDENTITY CARD
RATION BOOK
GAS MASK

ALSO any bank book, pensions payment order book, insurance cards, unemployment book, military registration documents, passport, insurance policies, securities and any ready money.

If your house will be left unoccupied, turn off gas, electricity and water supplies and make provision for animals and birds. Lock your house securely. Blinds should be left up, and if there is a telephone line, ask the telephone exchange to disconnect it.

Apply at the Local Council Offices for further information.

Private Car and Motor Cycle owners who have not licensed their vehicles and have no petrol coupons may be allowed to use their cars unlicensed for one journey only, and may apply to the Police for petrol coupons to enable them to secure sufficient petrol to journey to their destination.

ESSENTIAL WORKERS MUST STAY
particularly the following classes :—
Members of the Home Guard
Observer Corps
Coastguards, Coast Watchers and Lifeboat Crews
Police and Special Constabulary
Fire Brigade and Auxiliary Fire Service
A.R.P. and Casualty Services
Members of Local Authorities and their officials and employees
Workers on the land
Persons engaged on war work, and other essential services
Persons employed by contractors on defence work
Employees of water, sewerage, gas & electricity undertakings
Persons engaged in the supply and distribution of food
Workers on export trades
Doctors, Nurses and Chemists
Ministers of Religion
Government Employees
Employees of banks
Employees of transport undertakings,
namely railways, docks, canals, ferries,
and road transport (both passenger and goods).

When invasion is upon us it may be necessary to evacuate the remaining population of this and certain other towns. Evacuation would then be compulsory at short notice, in crowded trains, with scanty luggage, to destinations chosen by the Government. If you are not among the essential workers mentioned above, it is better to go now while the going is good.

Notice posted in 1940 advising residents on the South and East coasts to 'go now while the going is good'.

families and neighbourhoods alike, but to help the war effort by freeing up valuable space for war materials on the merchant shipping convoys.

In May 1940 the War Agricultural Executive Committees (WAEC) were given greater powers to ensure food production was maximised across the country. This process began with a quick but detailed survey of the country's farms to assess their produce potential and to decide if the farm was properly equipped and efficiently managed to fulfil that potential.

If there was a problem, the WAEC could arrange the loan of machinery

Right: A visitor's authorisation card that enabled those on essential business such as doctors or nurses to enter areas evacuated to minimal inhabitants because of the threat of invasion.
Below: A county constabulary constable (on one knee) and the Special Constables for a rural beat area, 1940.

AIR RAID PRECAUTIONS.

EVACUATION OF CIVIL POPULATION

VISITOR'S AUTHORISATION CARD

Stamp of Local Authority

NORTH WESTMORLAND R.D.C.

5 in List—HADDEN, BEST & Co., Ltd.,
West Harding Street, London, E.C.4.

Above: One of thousands of pillboxes erected across Britain to provide strong points for defending forces if Germany had made a successful invasion landing
Below: Men and boys working on a farm, 1940.

With imports greatly reduced, Britain had to maximise its home-grown produce and the 'Dig for Victory' scheme armed the public with useful information on how to do it.

or supply seed, fertilizers or lime on deferred terms if necessary; indeed, some farmers' productivity increased by 200–300 per cent. Farmers who failed to comply with cultivation orders could face a court appearance and a fine. If all else failed, the WAEC had the power to requisition the farmer's land; it would then be farmed under the auspices of the Committee or let to an approved tenant. There was no means of appeal against the decision of the War Agricultural Committee.

To increase the workforce on the land, town and city workers were encouraged to take their holiday helping with the harvest. Soldiers were also drafted in when required but the greatest contribution to work on the land in the war was made by the Women's Land Army (WLA). The WLA had proved their worth in the First World War and plans

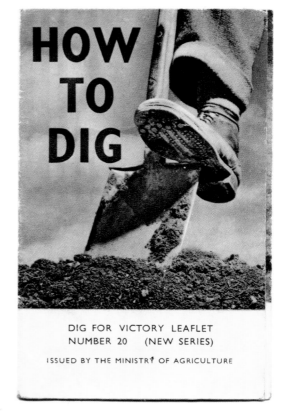

DIG FOR VICTORY LEAFLET
NUMBER 20   (NEW SERIES)

ISSUED BY THE MINISTRY OF AGRICULTURE

to raise them again were begun in 1938. On 1 June 1939 a grand recruitment campaign was launched. When war broke out in September 1939, some 17,000 volunteers had already registered with the fifty-two county offices, over 1,000 girls were dispatched immediately to placements on farms, and more girls joined during the massive recruitment campaign during the last week of April 1940.

WLA recruits came from a wide variety of backgrounds. There were both city and country girls among them, and most were young, often in their late teens, and officially joining 'for patriotic reasons'. Most will admit today that they chose the WLA in preference to military call-up or work in a munitions factory. Above all, Land Girls wanted to 'get away from it all' – a good enough reason to escape from humdrum jobs and stifling homes. Many female conscientious objectors also joined the WLA.

After sending off a written application, girls would be invited to an interview to assess their suitability. They were questioned by a board of at least two members of their local Agricultural Committee. The minimum age for enlistment in the WLA was seventeen and a half, but it appears that girls of seventeen were often accepted, and even sixteen-year-olds if they looked as if they were strong enough to do the work. The successful applicant would then be required to commit herself to the Land Army for the duration of the war. Girls could leave if they married, or transferred to other war work. The upper age limit seems to

Local ladies Mrs Baldry and Mrs Ling lending a hand on the land potato picking at Loudham, Suffolk, c. 1940.

Wartime recruitment poster for the Women's Land Army.

have been fifty, but many older women with relevant experience or social position occupied management positions in the organisation.

The girls worked the same day – from sun up to sundown – as the men on the farm. Many were not housed on the farms where they worked, but in hostels which were often country houses converted for the purpose supplemented by wooden huts. The girls had to get up very early to be bussed in, often on the back of a lorry or in an open trailer behind a tractor. Their work varied, like all farmwork, through the year, from ploughing and sowing and planting to harvesting. The most popular tasks were haymaking, looking after chickens, milking or working with livestock but, as ever, mucking out and the hard, dusty job of harvesting cereals were necessary too. Many farms were not able to replace their worn-out machinery, and some even had to resort to horse power and long redundant reaper-binders and hand ploughs when petrol was short. In fact, many farms still had not embraced anything other than horse power and crops such as sugar beet and carrots were lifted by hand.

The Women's Timber Corps (WTC) was formed as a separate arm of the WLA in April 1942. The 'Lumber Jills', as they were affectionately known, attended a four-week training course to learn the use of the saw, bill hook and axe. Once given their placement, much of their work was extremely hard, cutting wood for railway sleepers and pit props. The Timber Corps had 6,000 members nationally.

Right: A hand-tinted photograph of two Land Girls and the lambs under their care, *c.* 1942.
Below: Land Girls threshing grain, autumn 1942. (Getty Images)

Did you know?

At its peak in 1943, the WLA counted 80,000 active members in its ranks.

The WTC was disbanded in 1946 but 8,000 members of the WLA carried on through post-war austerity and rationing. The Women's Land Army was finally disbanded in 1950.

'The Friendly Invasion'

The arrival of the American Eighth Air Force bombers saw a number of airfields under construction for RAF bombers rescheduled for USAAF use and an unprecedented programme of new-build airfields rolled out across the country. Some of the extant RAF bases were also occupied by the USAAF. It was a massive undertaking; heavy bombers required concrete runways and hard standings, the individual costs of which often surpassed £1 million. Once completed, each airfield was occupied by a single Bombardment Group consisting of four flying Bombardment Squadrons; a squadron had an average compliment of twelve to sixteen bombers with 200 combat airmen. The total personnel on a bomber station varied between 2,000 and 3,000. With such a massive and sudden influx of foreign service personnel in the rural Eastern Counties of England, it is hardly surprising that the arrival of the Americans was known as 'The Friendly Invasion' and their bases as the 'Fields of Little America'. When setting off on their missions in daylight, twenty to forty heavy bombers would take off from a single airfield and would assemble into formation as they climbed to their operation altitude of 20,000 to 25,000 ft. Joined with other formations, they would form a division column of about 500–600 bombers; it was an impressive and unforgettable sight for anyone who saw them.

Many of the American servicemen got to know and be known in the surrounding towns and villages around their bases. Initially there were some problems; the British people had been at war since 1939, on the Home Front they had suffered air raids and rationing had bitten hard. The American servicemen had not experienced any of this and were seen by some as 'swanking' – they seemed to have a lot of money, their uniforms were 'flash' and if they were invited to tea, although their manners were good, they had no concept of moderation caused by rations. Women who had husbands serving abroad did not appreciate the advances of some of the Americans if they went to a dance; for some country folk, the culture shock was

Words and music for 'Comin' in on a Wing and a Prayer' (1943), one of the popular songs of the war, often associated with American aircrews limping home with damaged aircraft after a mission.

Above: Got any gum, chum? American servicemen from a nearby air base with local children in front of the Recruiting Sergeant pub, Horstead, Norfolk, 1944.
Right: A wartime wedding of an American serviceman and his British bride, c. 1944. Some 70,000 GI brides left the UK to start a new life in America with their servicemen husbands after the Second World War.

too much. Fights and missives such as 'Go home Yanks' were chalked on some walls in towns and villages near the bases. A sea change was needed; a guide had been produced for American servicemen coming to Britain and now information films were produced for personnel to learn more about British culture and how the war had affected them. Once a little time had passed, the natural curiosity of many country people and the warmth and good manners of the personnel saw friendships emerge that were to last for decades after the war.

6
War Production

In the same way that the land was maximised to ensure Britain did not starve, the sinking of so many merchant vessels meant that imports were severely curtailed and Britain had to maximise the output of its industries. Naturally, the production of hardware to fight the war such as aircraft, tanks, battleships, weaponry and ammunition were increased; as in the First World War many women were taken on to fill the jobs left by men serving in the military forces and provide workers for the new positions created by the expansions.

The small arms and filling factories were hives of industry with lathes and far more automated tools being used than ever before. Even the bigger industrial operations producing armoured fighting vehicles and battleships increasingly used prefabricated parts. This was not always without friction. Men who had served their time for years in the heavy and labour-intensive shipyards did not like the fact that one of the lighter but skilled jobs, and consequently one of the best paid jobs, was the riveter, a job done by

Above left: The Merchant Navy, so often forgotten, crossed thousands of miles of dangerous waters to keep Britain supplied during the Second World War.

Above right: Women munitions workers fitting fuses to 25 pounder gun shells.

Right: A woman welder at a Tyneside shipyard photographed by Cecil Beaton in 1943.
Below: Women war workers and volunteers taking a break for physical exercise at Herne Hill, June 1944. (Getty Images)

many of the new female members of the workforce. Differences aside, British shipyards produced a remarkable 700 warships, 5,000 smaller craft and 4.5 million tons of merchant shipping between 1939 and June 1944.

Did you know?

The workforce of 1.25 million people working in munitions production in 1939 had increased to 8.5 million by 1943.

None of this would have been possible without the fuel that powered all British heavy industries, provided the main supply of solid fuels in homes and businesses, and put the fire in the belly of British warships – coal. The industry is famed for the 'Bevin Boy' scheme of 1943 developed by Minister of Labour Ernest Bevin; the scheme saw to it that conscripted men (unless they had special skills suitable for aircrew or submarines) were balloted and as a result 21,000 men were sent down mines instead of to the fighting forces. It should be remembered, however, that as many men worked hard in the mines before and continued to do so during the war, and that many young lads, some as young as thirteen, volunteered to train and work down the pits.

Boys, some as young as fourteen, hear about the coal cutter from miner Mr P. K. Wilson at a training pit at Ashington, Northumberland, May 1940. (Science and Society Picture Library)

Did you know?

Over 700,000 men worked in the coal industry during the Second World War.

Away from heavy industry, many factories were also turned over to war production, making a huge array of goods for the war effort from uniforms, army boots and buttons to shrapnel helmets, parachutes, medical supplies and tinned foods.

Salvage

Every piece of scrap and redundant material that could be re-used for war production had its own salvage collection: it was the nation's first introduction to recycling on a massive scale. The removal of iron railings deemed 'unnecessary' under Regulation 50 of the Defence (General) Regulations, 1939, was not all it seemed. The idea was that they would be melted down for munitions but it was formally admitted in Parliament as early as 1943 that the wrought iron was 'found unsuitable' for those purposes and was discreetly dumped in landfill and in the sea. It was argued later that the whole operation had been a morale building exercise aimed at uniting the country by a visible shared act. Later salvage efforts were put to far more practical use.

Girl Guides and their grand paper salvage collection, August 1940.

I need your **SCRAP METAL**

PUT OUT YOUR SCRAP METAL FOR SALVAGE
to make Tanks · Guns · Ships · Shells · Bombs
Machine Guns · Grenades · Cartridges · Bullets
Mines · Steel Helmets · Torpedoes · Rifles etc.

On a domestic level most gardens had at least three containers, one for each of the 'big three' salvage materials: paper, bones and rags. Paper was used in munitions to make cartridge boxes, wads, mortar bomb carriers, interior components for mines and shooting targets. Paper was also used in the manufacture of prefabricated buildings and construction: one ton of paper jointing was used in every mile of concrete runway. Posters were quick to depict dramatic battle scenes or images of rugged servicemen calling for all the various elements of salvage; in the case of paper they were emblazoned with statements like '60 cigarette cartons make one bomb container' and '20 periodicals make one seat for a pilot'. Bones went to make glue and fertilizer and soap, while rags

Left: On this poster a tank commander calls for scrap metal for munitions, *c.* 1944.
Below: Aluminium pots, pans and kettles collected for salvage, 1940.

could be used to make uniforms, camouflage netting, roofing felt, gun wadding, rags to wipe engines and machinery in production and repair, even maps and charts.

There would also be a bucket for kitchen scraps such as potato peelings and other food waste to feed pigs and poultry. But as rationing bit harder, these became sparse as householders were encouraged to use many parts of vegetables and meat that would often have been discarded in peacetime.

There were also nationwide schemes to collect scrap aluminium to be melted down to make aircraft, tin cans to be melted down and used in war production (including making tin cans) and even rubber which, although it was not melted down, could be shaped and re-used as helmet liners and a host of small parts for military equipment carried by the fighting forces.

'Salvage dumps' where there were large bins to collect paper, bones, rags and metal were common sights in every town and city, where the materials would be collected by local councils and removed to processing centres by ministry contractors. The day-to-day running of salvage collections and 'salvage drives', where there was a focus on one particular salvageable material such as aluminium or paper, was often carried out or assisted by members of the WI and WVS and youth organisations such as Boys Scouts, Girl Guides and young people's volunteer working groups known as 'Cogs', who would help collect salvage and earn a Junior Salvage Steward badge for their efforts.

Charity Collections, Schemes and Drives

The huge contribution of those at home who knitted 'comforts' for our fighting forces is often forgotten. Many schemes began on a local level with women coming together to knit gloves, fingerless mittens, socks, balaclavas and scarves for lads serving abroad. The WIs, WVS and other women's groups and Church-based women's societies soon joined in, with more organised drives to create thousands of knitted goods that were sent to our fighting forces all over the world. The International Red Cross and Order of St John, also drew in the home knitters to supply knitted goods for hospitals, convalescent troops and prisoners of war.

There was a huge variety of street collections to raise funds for wartime causes on both local and national levels. Among the most prominent were the Joint War Organisation of the British

One of numerous wartime knitting patterns for service 'comforts'.

MORE 'COMFORTS' FOR THE FORCES

KNITTED IN

Sirdar
WOOLS

LEAFLET No. 869. PRICE 3ᴰ.

Instructions for making:
COMBINED HELMET AND SCARF
SOCKS · GLOVES
SERVICE HELMET

HARRAP BROS. (SIRDAR WOOLS) LIMITED · WAKEFIELD

Above: Women came together in all sorts of groups, from Women's Institutes to locally raised wartime groups, to knit 'comforts' for service personnel.

Left: Badge given as a token of thanks to those who knitted garments for the Royal Navy.

Red Cross Society and Order of St John, who raised money predominantly for providing first aid posts, casualty clearing stations and ambulance services to the nation and for their work supporting prisoners of war with supplies, comforts and food parcels all over the world. The RSPCA were well supported for their ARP work for animals. The YMCA collected to raise money for its mobile canteens that supplied very welcome cups of tea and snacks not only in bombed cities and towns but also to isolated troops manning gun emplacements and searchlights far from their base canteens. Charities realised they were often duplicating work and knew a big, combined drive across a city or town would yield bigger results and very soon War Charities Weeks were being held across the country.

There were also great drives for the British public to dig through their cupboards to find things to help the fighting forces; for example, the Ministry of Supply put out a request for 125,000 pairs of binoculars to be given or sold to them via their authorised collection agents (usually a local optician). People were also asked to donate books and reading materials for prisoners of war and sailors at sea, to find clothes for evacuees as they grew out of their old ones and donate clothes and blankets for those who had been bombed out of their homes during the Blitz.

The biggest national efforts were for National Savings and they raised millions of pounds, beginning with Beaverbrook's Spitfire Week in 1940, then War Weapons Week (1941), Warship Week (1942), Wings for Victory (1943) and Salute the Soldier (1944). Each of these weeks would see a city or town filled with public events, military parades and concerts. The schemes were geared towards raising money to buy specific things such as 100 four-engine bombers, a tank or a Spitfire's thermometer.

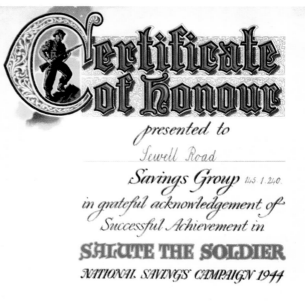

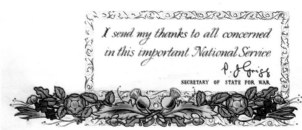

The 'Salute the Soldier' campaign urged the British public to invest in National Savings in 1944 to enable one last big push to 'finish the job.'

7
Rations and Fashions

Food

In 1939 less than a third of the food available in Britain was produced at home. In the opening years of the war the U-boat campaign that sank thousands of tonnes of merchant vessels and huge areas of mined sea channels caused vital supplies of sugar, fruit, cereals and meat to be dramatically reduced.

Rationing in Britain began on 8 January 1940 with bacon, butter and sugar. Everyone had been issued a ration book; this did not entitle the holder to free food but it did entitle the bearer to their allocated share or ration.

Any animal to be slaughtered by a butcher had to be approved according to government quotas. Over-the-counter meat was allocated by price (to the value of 1s 2d) so cheaper cuts became popular. Sausages were not rationed but were more difficult to obtain and contained less meat to make them go further. Offal was in great demand and more unusual meats such as turbot, whale and horse made occasional appearances. There was no restriction on rabbits and they certainly became a meat staple in country areas where poaching became rife. Pig clubs, where a group of people on a street would feed and raise a pig until it was of suitable size for slaughter, became a popular activity and more people than ever bred rabbits and kept chickens.

Did you know?

The spirit of husbandry and allotments (from 815,000 plots pre-war to 1.4 million) saw a huge expansion in the number of youngsters joining Young Farmers' Clubs, where they could attend proficiency courses in a variety of agrarian skills.

During the war rationing varied as some supplies became more sparse than others. A typical weekly allowance of rationed food for one person would be: one fresh egg; 4 oz margarine and bacon (about four rashers); 2 oz butter and tea; 1 oz cheese; and 8 oz sugar. With such a restricted diet children, pregnant women and the sick were allocated extra rations of milk and concentrated orange juice. Children would also be given cod liver oil and 'Virol', a sickly sweet extract of malt, to make sure they got the vitamins they needed. Sweets were soon rationed too at 12 oz (350 g) every four weeks.

The Ministry of Food did its best to produce a helpful series of Food Facts booklets and recipe pamphlets to make meals go a bit further and be more interesting. Some fruits became very such as oranges; some children aged around eight years old, when given one of the rarities, were seen biting into them like apples. Bananas were among the rarest fruits so advice was given in wartime recipe books on how to make 'mock banana' using mashed parsnips and banana essence. Carrots replaced sugar in tarts and powdered egg, corned beef and Spam became household mainstays during the course of the war.

Above: Food Ration Book and cardboard holder given away with the compliments of sugar producers Tate & Lyle, 1941.
Right: The cockney charwomen comedy characters Gert and Daisy, created by Doris and Elsie Waters, appeared on radio, film, in magazines and books to convey a variety of important government messages and schemes to the general public during the Second World War.

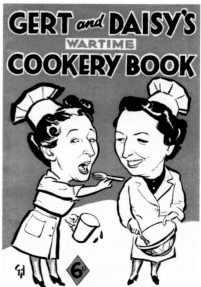

Did you know?

Woolton Pie, the layered vegetable pie claimed to be just as satisfying as one with meat in it, was named after the avuncular Lord Woolton, Minister of Food.

The Ministry of Food produced 'Kitchen Front' features on radio advising the public of dos and don'ts of food in wartime. Marguerite Patten's cooking tips on the Home Service drew 6 million listeners a day and 'Food Flashes' appeared in cinemas between 1942 and 1946. Some of these did raise a laugh and were enjoyed because audiences knew and liked some of the characters, like the cockney charwomen characters Gert and Daisy, created by Doris and Elsie Waters.

Did you know?

In 1939 the Women's Institute (WI) had mobilised its membership of 5,270 branches (with 331,612 members) onto a war footing and was the backbone of the war effort on the Home Front.

To ensure we all kept well fed, the WI National Executive launched the Produce Guild to encourage home production of food. By arrangement with the Ministry of Food, 434 tons of sugar were issued to WI branches for preserving purposes and much fruit that would otherwise have been wasted was saved. When the U-boat menace tightened its grip on shipping and imports and rationing was first introduced, the women of the WI took it in their stride. The Women's Institute arranged special talks and demonstrations for its membership as well as publishing recipes in its magazine and giving public lectures about cooking on rations, food substitutes, pickling and bottling. So

Potato Pete was a cartoon character used to promote a variety of recipes using wartime vegetable staples.

it came as no surprise when the NFWI began to administer the Ministry of Food's fruit preservation scheme and jam making centres (which also produced chutneys and bottled fruit) were established across the country, many of them run or staffed by WI members. By 1941 it was reported the scheme had produced some 1,630 tons of preserves.

Restaurants were exempt from rationing, which led to a certain amount of resentment as the more affluent could supplement their food allowance by eating out. To restrict this, certain rules were put into force. No meal could cost more than 5 shillings; no meal could consist of more than three courses, and meat and fish could not be served at the same sitting. 'Community Feeding Centres', later re-named British Restaurants, were set up by the Ministry of Food across the country. Run by local committees on a non-profit-making basis, meals in British Restaurants came with their own restrictions. No customer could be served with a meal of more than one serving of meat, fish, game, poultry, eggs or cheese purchased for a maximum price of 9*d* or less. The standard of food was very dependent on the skill of the cooks and what foodstuffs were available; when all other meat sources were drying up, there was always rabbit and wonders were often achieved with its creative use. Some restaurants certainly had their sense of humour; one dish occasionally seen chalked on a restaurant blackboard promised 'Sea Pie – buy it and See what is in it!'

Clothes

The price of clothing shot up by 18 per cent in the first four months of the war but clothes were still available, while stocks lasted. The Board of Trade carefully considered the pros and cons of clothes rationing and it was finally introduced in 1941 with spare margarine coupons in a standard food ration book used for the first issue of twenty-six coupons. The first clothing ration books were introduced in 1942. Rationed clothing was purchased using a combination of coupons and money. Each person was allocated sixty-six coupons a year, which would roughly equate to a complete new outfit. Babies and growing children posed a problem for families trying to manage their precious coupons. New mothers were given an extra fifty coupons for baby clothes.

There was a real concern in government that a lack of interest in personal appearance could be a sign of low morale and as a result

The Drapers' Record magazine, September 1939, the last pre-war season of the latest fashions.

Did you know?

The first 'Utility' clothes went on sale in 1942. Every garment was marked with the CC41 stamp or label to denote they were made from a limited range of quality-controlled fabrics. They would also be sold at regulated prices so that they could be affordable for all.

Practical for women on war work and a refreshing dash of colour, the headscarf came into its own during the Second World War.

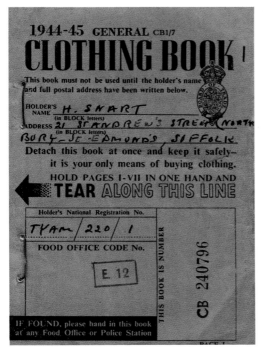

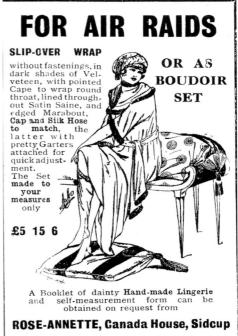

Above left: Clothing Ration Book, 1944–45. Rationing for clothes was introduced on 1 June 1941 and only ended in March 1949.

Above right: Fashions tried to accommodate the vagaries of war with developments such as siren suits and this slip-over wrap for air raids, 1940.

they decided to continue to manufacture cosmetics, albeit in reduced quantities. Make-up and hairstyles took on an increased importance. With some make-up on and a smart hairstyle, protected by a fine, colourful scarf or remodelled hat with accessories or even a new one (hats were not rationed but they were harder to come by and subject to purchase tax as 'luxury items'), a woman could still feel well dressed and stylish even if her clothes were from last season and her stockings darned. Women's magazines appreciated this was the situation and published features about how to adjust clothes to reflect the latest vogue – it was the patriotic thing to do. The Board of Trade's leaflets featuring the character Mrs Sew and Sew also gave advise on how to repair, darn and make clothes.

Due to shortages of silk in wartime, many women opted to get married in a smart suit instead, and it could easily be worn again afterwards. Other girls borrowed pre-war wedding dresses (some dresses were used for numerous marriages) or even had them made out of parachute silk obtained from rescue crews or 'a man who knew someone'. Parachute silk was actually made from rayon or nylon and was widely available from 1945, when surplus stocks not used in wartime hit the market, and was used for more wedding dresses and to make underwear.

Above left: The Board of Trade's 'Make Do and Mend' scheme fronted by the ragdoll character Mrs Sew and Sew showed and encouraged people to make and repair.

Above right: The 'CC 41' stamp used to denote Utility items made from government-controlled materials that guaranteed quality and value in clothes, fabric products and furniture.

Left: *Stitchcraft* magazine was halved from its pre-war size due to paper shortages but it carried on with colour covers and all manner of fashion tips and patterns through the war years.

A wartime wedding, c. 1942. By the middle war years clothes rationing and short supplies of silk saw many women get married in borrowed pre-war wedding dresses, dresses made from parachute silk 'acquired' by a variety of means, or in their best civilian clothes.

Once married, those setting up a new home together after 1943 would have encountered the Utility scheme as it expanded beyond clothing and shoes to include household textiles, crockery, bedding and furniture. Between 1943 and 1946 all furniture made for civilian use had to be made to set Utility designs and a permit would have been required to make a purchase. Some couples made their Utility furniture last their entire married life.

8
Victory

As Allied progress was made from the D-Day landings in June 1944 the reason for a Home Guard diminished and inevitably the days of the organisation were numbered. On 30 August 1944 the War Office issued Instructions for Standing Down the Home Guard and a formal notice circulated in October gave notification that the Home Guard was to stand down from active duties in November 1944. Parades and march-pasts were held to mark the occasion as each battalion stood down. Civil Defence, WVS, WLA, Red Cross and St John Ambulance units hung on to the end of the war and, although greatly reduced in numbers, they carried on in peacetime roles. In the immediate aftermath of the war 75 per cent of the full-time officers, men and women of the National Fire Service went back to their civilian occupations and roles. The Fire Services Act became law on 31 July 1947, which meant the NFS was unscrambled with effect from 1 April 1948 and the administration of fire brigades was handed over to counties and boroughs again.

VE Day arrived on 8 May 1945 with the announcement by Prime Minister Winston Churchill that, 'We may allow ourselves a brief period of rejoicing.' Streets and market places rapidly filled with revellers in both civvies and uniforms of every hue and celebrations were held across the country as streets dusted off the coronation bunting and local folks clubbed

One of the street parties held across Britain to celebrate VE Day, 8 May 1945, but it would not be until 15 August that final victory in the Far East could be declared and VJ Day celebrated.

together to pool their ration coupons to get a few treats for the children at their street party. Most children had a great time and so did many adults, but look closer at the faces of many ladies – mothers, sisters, wives and girlfriends; their smiles are not as wide as they might be because their special relative is not there to share the day. For many families, their loved one's fight was still going on in the Far East in India and Burma, or perhaps the men waited for freedom from captivity in the hands of the Japanese, a freedom that would only be made possible by the defeat of Japan. Six days after the United States dropped atomic bombs on Hiroshima and Nagasaki, on 15 August 1945, Japan announced its surrender to the Allied powers and the soldiers and captives of the Far East could begin to look forward to making the long journey home again.

Delays due to the regulations in 'demob' release schemes and spaces available on shipping prevented many men in the Far East from returning until 1946. For some of those called up late in the war, the situation was similar in Germany and they ended up serving in the occupation forces. A number of British corps and units were also present when some of the major concentration camps were opened. For many it was the sights they saw in the camps that lingered in their nightmares. With the return of our heroes special dinners and welcome home events were held and the men tried to settle back into civvy life. For some the reunion with children they had not seen for years and vice versa proved difficult, but then they were fortunate; there were some children who never saw Daddy again.

9
What Now?

Getting Involved

Membership of a society is not essential to learning more about the Home Front during the Second World War but it can be a great way to make contacts, help you find out more

The country's return to Civvy Street was celebrated on the cover of *Woman and Home's* Christmas edition, December 1945.

ways you can get involved, and find people who share the same interest in the subjects that you do. People who are new to the subject should not feel intimidated: we all had to start somewhere and no good historian ever stops learning. I would also suggest you look at some online forums or social media groups to see what Second World War projects and exhibitions are going on in your area. There are also a growing number of large and small-scale 1940s events held across Great Britain and these can be good places to see what groups are out there for yourself and have a chat face to face.

Collecting

Memorabilia, uniforms, badges and insignia from the British Home Front in the Second World War can still be found at good quality militaria fairs today (as well as at antiques fairs, car boot sales and flea markets). Please be aware that cap badges have been re-struck and cloth insignia, uniforms and equipment have been reproduced for re-enactors but these can be aged and sold as originals so I would urge caution and advise if you are going to start buying such collectables, start at militaria fairs and ask the fair organiser to direct you to the longest established badge or militaria dealers; there has to be a reason why they have been around so long. Once you have purchased a few reasonably priced original items, keep on with your research learning what to look for in genuine 1940s collectables, and your confidence will grow. Don't let your heart rule your head; wanting an item you fear may be a reproduction to be authentic will not make it the real deal, neither does paying a big price for it. Never feel pressured to make a purchase. We have all passed over items we wish we had bought. Above all, take your time, learn well and enjoy collecting and researching the memorabilia of the British Home Front during The Second World War.

Here are three reliable online dealers I personally recommend:

Sally Bosley's Badge Shop http://sallybosleysbadgeshop.com
Home Front Collection www.homefrontcollection.com
Britton's Badges www.brittonsbadges.co.uk

Further Reading

Briggs, Susan, *Keep Smiling Through* (Weidenfield & Nicholson 1975)
Calder, Angus, *The People's War* (Pimlico 1969)
Collier, Basil, *The Battle of the V-Weapons, 1944–45* (Elmfield 1964)
Fleming, Peter, *Invasion 1940* (Hart-Davis 1957)
Freeman, Roger, *The Mighty Eighth* (Arms & Armour 1989)
Grant, Ian and Maddren, Nicholas, *The Countryside at War* (Jupiter 1975)
Graves, Charles, *The Home Guard of Britain* (Hutchinson 1943)
Longmate, Norman, *How We Lived Then: A History of Everyday Life during the Second World War* (Hutchinson 1971)
Ramsey, Winston G. (ed.), *The Blitz Then and Now September 1939 – September 1940* (After the Battle 1987)
Ramsey, Winston G. (ed.), *The Blitz Then and Now September 1940 – May 1941* (After the Battle 1988)
Ramsey, Winston G. (ed.), *The Blitz Then and Now May 1941 – May 1945* (After the Battle 1987)
Storey, Neil, R., *The Home Guard* (Shire 2009)

The Times, *British War Production 1939–1945* (Times Publishing Co. 1945)
Tillett, Iris, *The Cinderella Army* (Tillett 1988)
Warwicker, John, *Churchill's Underground Army* (Frontline 2008)
Wills, Henry, *Pillboxes, A Study of UK Defences 1940* (Leo Cooper 1985)

Places to Visit

Imperial War Museum, Lambeth Road, London, SE1 6HZ
Established at the end of the First World War as Britain's national war museum, it's a great place to start your journey learning about life in the Second World War.

Imperial War Museum (North), The Quays, Trafford Wharf Road, Manchester, M17 1TZ
IWM (North) has powerful displays relating how war affects people's lives and a good section of displays covering a variety of aspects of the Second World War. See their website for their current temporary exhibitions: www.iwm.org.uk/visits/iwm-north.

Web Resources

There has been a great interest in the Second World War Home Front for years; look online for projects in your local area. The information quality can, however, be variable so I would recommend starting any research with some strong foundations by engaging with established national collections and archives:

www.iwm.org.uk/collections
Imperial War Museum Collections are a superb resource for both photographs and memorabilia relating to soldiers of the Second World War. Explore the whole IWM site for events and other connections.

www.nationalarchives.gov.uk/help-with-your-research/research-guides/second-world-war/
The National Archives offers a vast resource for anyone researching life and organisations on the Home Front during the Second World War and provides some useful online guides.

www.bbc.co.uk/history/ww2peopleswar/
WW2 People's War is an online archive of Second World War memories written by the public, gathered by the BBC.

www.cwgc.org/
The Commonwealth War Graves Commission is an invaluable site to help you trace civilian war dead of the Second World War. Their website also has useful information about upcoming anniversaries and commemorations.